IMAGES
of America

SEWARD COUNTY

The Seward County Courthouse still stands after over 115 years. Few remember that the smokestack across Highway 34 to the south was once part of the heating system for the courthouse. The heat came through a tunnel underground. Imagine waiting on the lawn on a hot summer day to hear through the open windows the verdict of the courts or the judge shooting the pigeons out of the tower. People from all the communities in Seward County came here to pay their taxes, obtain their licenses, and seek justice. (Courtesy of the Seward County Historical Society.)

On the Cover: Albert Flowerday farmed about four miles north of Seward. Although he never had more than an eighth-grade formal education, he was director of the school board of District 28. He is seen here in one of his wheat fields in 1946. (Courtesy of Elaine Flowerday Vrana.)

IMAGES
of America

SEWARD COUNTY

Pat Coldiron

ARCADIA
PUBLISHING

ISBN 978-1-4671-0600-9

Published by Arcadia Publishing
Charleston, South Carolina

Printed in the United States of America

Library of Congress Control Number: 2020944377

For all general information, please contact Arcadia Publishing:
Telephone 843-853-2070
Fax 843-853-0044
E-mail sales@arcadiapublishing.com
For customer service and orders:
Toll-Free 1-888-313-2665

Visit us on the Internet at www.arcadiapublishing.com

Contents

ACKNOWLEDGMENTS

A sincere and heartfelt thank-you to the Seward County Historical Society for its assistance and support in researching and locating many of the photographs in this history. The librarian at the museum, Diane Rohren, was unfailing in her assistance. This was a magnificent demonstration by residents from every corner of the county volunteering their time and knowledge in gathering and sharing individual and family photographs and memories. Everyone did their utmost to document and check the details for each entry. However, we know that over 150 years over 500 square miles of the prairie, there might be differences in documentation. This was an experience of becoming enchanted with each community as it was researched, and each person's contribution is recognized and appreciated.

INTRODUCTION

Our way led across the Middle Creek hills and the great plains to the west, and just as the bright sun was sinking behind the western hills, there opened to our view the grand valley of the North Blue, with its long lines of timber stretching far away to the southward and northward, and the diverging lines of the Lincoln Creek and Plum Creek. Oh! To us it was a grander view than Moses had from Pisgah's top! It was an enchanting and rapturous scene. We said in our heart, "this is the place we long have sought!"

—W.W. Cox

Seward County is made up of 576 square miles and is found in the lower southeast corner of Nebraska, about 25 miles west of Lincoln. It was included in the Louisiana Purchase of 1808. Its current boundaries were established in 1856, when Nebraska was still a territory. Initially named Greene County, in 1862, the county was renamed after William Seward, a leading antislavery politician and secretary of state in the Lincoln administration. Its population at this time was 25. The county is primarily agricultural.

Before 1869, judicial matters for Seward County were handled in Lancaster County. In October 1865, Seward County began the process of political organization with the election of its first board of county commissioners. Only 24 votes were cast. The first district court met in Milford in November 1869, with George B. Lake the first judge. Thomas West was the first county clerk, and Frank Ellsworth was the first district attorney. Beginning in the spring of 1871, the district court met in Seward.

Daniel Morgan was the first settler in 1858 along the Big Blue River (although he later relocated), with Thomas West settling shortly after on the West Blue River. J.L. Davison opened a ranch west of the Camden bridge in 1862, and W.J. Thompson settled about the same time near the mouth of Walnut Creek. In the same fall, A.J. Wallingford started his ranch at the old Camden bridge and John Fouse started his at the mouth of Beaver Creek. Daniel Millspaw opened a road ranch a little west near the York County line. Job Reynolds and Samuel Long settled on the North Blue River in the spring of 1863, and C.J. Neihardt, T.L. Rogers, Jesse Johnson, and David Barton made a settlement on the South Blue in 1864. Robert T. Gale made the first homestead entry on January 2, 1863. The Homestead Act took effect on January 1, 1863. Gale's entry was No. 7.

Except for a brief visit by Cortez in the 16th century, the tall grasses of the prairie in and around Seward County existed pretty much in solitude, traversed only occasionally by Native Americans. With the implementation of the Homestead Act, Civil War veterans being compensated in land in lieu of cash, and the building of the railroads, the influx began.

Initially, settlers made their way into Seward County via the freight trails in the late 1850s and early 1860s. A rail line was built in 1873 from Lincoln to Seward through the new railroad community of Germantown/Garland and then extended west. Following this track, Tamora and Utica were established. The second rail line was laid with Pleasant Dale, Ruby, and Staplehurst along the way, and in 1887, the third track was built, with Cordova, Beaver Crossing, Goehner, and Bee being platted.

It is difficult to imagine the hardships those early settlers endured. They left established homes in the eastern United States or Europe and traveled out here mostly on foot accompanied by their wagons and teams of oxen, mules, or horses. Upon arrival, they sought refuge in a dugout in the side of a hill or a house made of chunks of sod. If they were lucky and timber was nearby, they built a log cabin. They had to deal with hunger, fires, snakes, fear, loneliness, and disease. These initial settlers paid an extraordinary price to take a chance on the prairie, and in 10 short years, the railroad changed their lives by connecting them with the rest of the world.

One

Beaver Crossing

This daguerreotype image was made in 1866 by one of a party of Mormons traveling from Illinois to Utah. It shows the Roland Reed homestead, which was on the California trail. For years after, these buildings stood on land two and a half miles west of Beaver Crossing. According to a relative in the 1930s, Roland Reed and his daughter Eva stand together at right, with Mrs. Reed to their right. Charlie and Alice Reed stand near center, and Jim Anderson is standing near the well. W.A. Reed sits on the horse, and Horatio Reed holds the bridle of the other horse. John Reed stands in the door. In 1871, a new flour mill was built on the Blue River, and T.H. Tisdale moved his store to the new location about four miles from the original crossing. The town was platted in 1875. (Courtesy of the Nebraska State Historical Society.)

In 1862, John Leonard made a freighting trip from Nebraska City to the western plains. On his return trip, he camped on Beaver Creek along with his wagon and two yokes of oxen. He met some campers from the east who said they were drafting all available men for service in the Civil War. Leonard decided to stay right there, build a ranch, and start supplying travelers. A ranch in those days actually was a hotel, restaurant, store, and post office. His place was on the north side of Beaver Creek and was the first settlement in L precinct. About 1864, Amos Reed bought the land and ranch from Leonard. Reed was the governor of Utah and purchased 1,400 acres of government land at $1.25 an acre. He offered his brother Roland 140 acres to come out from Pennsylvania and settle there. Daniel Millspaw had settled at the west end of Beaver Crossing in a two-room cabin with his wife and daughter. When the Reeds arrived, they added groceries, and the post office was called Beaver Crossing. (Courtesy of Lori Anderson.)

With the discovery of the flowing wells, residents began irrigating gardens, fruit orchards, and potatoes. With water and the high productivity of the soil, truck farming and fruit growing were especially profitable. In 1904, there were 96 railcars, each containing 500 bushels of potatoes, shipped from the community. This photograph was taken during the potato harvest of 1915 on the Frank Eisenbarth farm. They also grew fields of cabbage and strawberries. (Courtesy of the Seward County Historical Society.)

Stacking prairie hay was a tough job and developed into a fine skill. Farmers fill the big forks full, the team backs up, and at a certain point, it is let go, flinging the hay on top of the growing stack. Another man on top levels it as it falls. The field was mown beforehand by a horse-drawn sickle mower and left to dry in the field. (Courtesy of the Seward County Historical Society.)

In 1895, Beaver Crossing formed a stock company for the purpose of promoting an annual picnic. The picnics were held along the river with baseball games, music, speakers, and a parade. In 1908, about 5,000 people attended, and in 1912, more than 7,000 attended. (Courtesy of the Seward County Historical Society.)

The Beaver Crossing Roller Mill was built on the Blue River in 1871. The farmers brought their grain to the mill and waited for their wheat or corn to be ground into flour. During peak production, 60 barrels of flour and 1,000 bushels of corn per day were produced. With the coming of World War I, the mill ceased operation in 1917 and stood idle until 1935, when it was salvaged. (Courtesy of the Seward County Historical Society.)

In about 1893–1895, there was a severe drought. DeWitt Eager had a well in his store. The water from this well became impure, so he hired Ray Virgin to sink the well deeper to find better water. Finally, the bottom seemed to fall out, and water rushed up with such force that the cellar was half full before anyone realized what was happening. Before long, many others were digging for these wonderful wells. Pictured is a frozen well. (Courtesy of the Seward County Historical Society.)

In 1910, a huge swimming pool was built in the Beaver Crossing park fed by flowing wells. People from miles around came on Sunday afternoons; sometimes, up to 900 people enjoyed the pool. No one was allowed in without a bathing suit. It was used until 1943, but as the men were called to service during World War II, a caretaker was not available. Finally, in 1962, it was drained and filled in. (Courtesy of the Seward County Historical Society.)

Dr. Doty and his family are pictured out and about. According to Don Danskin, beginning in the 1920s, homes and stores were furnished with cold running water from the artesian wells. Common places of interest at that time were the watering trough and the hitching post on Main Street. Also popular were Darling's livery stable, the skating rink, the blacksmith shop, Colson's sprinkling wagon for the dirt roads, the park and swimming pool, the Eager Building, the theater, the little frame schoolhouse, and the two-story, bell-towered high school. These days were punctuated by colorful parades opening the annual picnic, Chautauqua programs, the occasional flooding of the Blue River, and Halloween pranks. People also saw the first radios, the first use of trucks in transporting grain to elevators, and the landing of Earl Smiley's airplane in the cemetery. This new day brought such luxuries as sliced bread, balloon tires, leaded gasoline, and ice-cream cones. Roads were being graveled, and good roads meant an expanded shopping area. (Courtesy of the Seward County Historical Society.)

T.H. Tisdale, the third postmaster, moved his store and the post office from its original site near Beaver Creek to the present site of Beaver Crossing. Tisdale was known for his unique distribution of the mail. Upon its arrival, he would call out peoples' names (they all gathered there on mail day) and then toss their letter or package to them. In 1887, a total of 150 new Morris keyless lock boxes were ordered from Seward. (Courtesy of the Seward County Historical Society.)

Citizens State Bank was formed in 1905, and the building of cement blocks (made by the Beaver Crossing Cement Block Company) was erected. This bank, along with the Beaver Crossing State Bank, closed in 1933 in the Depression. The building was then used as a post office. As seen in this 1940s image, friends gathered by the water fountain to discuss world affairs. (Courtesy of the Seward County Historical Society.)

Erle Smiley committed himself to excel in anything he set his mind to, demonstrated initially as he judged his first poultry show at the Seward County Fair in 1907 when he was 17. In 1915, he established the Rose Lawn Poultry Farm near Beaver Crossing. He then showed chickens at meets in London, Boston, and New York City, later becoming a worldwide judge himself. He judged at Madison Square Garden, Philadelphia, the Chicago World's Fair, Los Angeles, Hawaii, and Canada. In the 1920s, he established the Smiley Hatchery in Seward. He and Harold Davisson partnered to tear down the old mill in Beaver Crossing to repurpose the lumber. Smiley used it for his new venture, a trout hatchery and water gardens in Beaver Crossing. Davisson used his share to start his own hatchery in Seward. Smiley was also an accomplished pilot. The World War I-era airplane below bears the logo of his Rose Lawn Poultry Farm. (Both, courtesy of Marilyn Smiley Schulz.)

Smiley, pictured here standing on the wheel of the airplane, enlisted in the military in 1917 as a flying cadet. He was commissioned a second lieutenant in the air service and was assigned as a flight instructor at March Field in California. After his discharge, he engaged in commercial flying and brought home a Curtiss JN-4 "Jenny" biplane, becoming one of the first barnstormers in the Midwest. Smiley was instrumental in the organization of the local unit of the National Guard. In 1912, he was elected to the state legislature, where he proposed legislation to regulate flying to make travel safer. (Courtesy of Marilyn Smiley Schulz.)

Smiley developed his water gardens into the largest privately owned commercial water garden in the world. During this time, he had the largest water lily and water plant collection in existence. His son-in-law Pee Wee Schulz tells how there were so many bullfrogs around the gardens that they would hunt them and layer them on ice, selling truckloads to the Cornhusker Hotel in Lincoln. (Both, courtesy of Marilyn Smiley Schulz.)

By the 1920s, Beaver Crossing had two hospitals, several saloons, a lumber and coal company, two banks, a blacksmith, and five churches along with retail shops and several grocery stores. The population was 543. The original building for the Beaver Crossing hardware store was erected in 1890 at 808 Dimery Street. A notice in the newspaper in 1893 read, "If the young lady who lost a pocketbook containing $5.00 and a recipe for removing freckles while in the drug store buying a pound of baking powder for 25 cents will call and accurately describe same, it will be returned and the recipe filled free of charge." In the 1940s, the business was a combination hardware store and implement dealer. The owner from 1955 to 1989 sold it to Kenny Pankoke and his father, Dean Pankoke. Kenny then became the sole owner in 1992. (Courtesy of Branden Mares.)

Kenny Pankoke and his wife, Christy, purchased the lot next to the building and began expanding. Dean still helped out in the store, even though his eyesight was failing. His local customers would just write in the account book what they had purchased, and a bill was sent out at the end of the month. In 2005, the store again expanded to the west, and in 2018 added a line of home décor. In 2014, nearly 40 percent of the business was destroyed in the "Mother's Day Tornado" that swept through the area. They rebuilt, and as of 2019, the store covers over 15,000 square feet. This business in rural Nebraska is still thriving and meeting its community's needs after 130 years. (Courtesy of Linda Jacox.)

Because of the good soil and the plentiful flowing wells in this valley near the Blue River, truck gardening thrived along with the fishery. In 1936, the town of Beaver Crossing formed the first co-op organization of tomato producers in the United States. It was not until mid-1942, however, that any actual canning was done. In July 1942, a total of 229 tons of tomatoes were canned and processed. Thirty-three percent of over 8,000 cans of tomatoes were sold to the US government, and the rest was sold for civilian use. In 1943, it expanded to the canning of green beans (over 43,000 cans). The co-op employed over 30 people during the season. When they put the operation together, the peeling tables were made out of old bed frames welded together, and cooking vats were handmade. Eighty acres of tomatoes were planted for the first year. Some of the equipment was made at the Defense School in Milford. It was impossible to keep it going during World War II because of the shortage of manpower. The tomato cannery is pictured here. (Courtesy of Branden Mares.)

The Mother's Day Tornado of 2014 was devastating to Beaver Crossing. Over 30 homes were either lost or damaged. Once again, Nebraska's resilience showed through. In a year's time, more than 20 homes and businesses were repaired and restored. The tornado touched down around 5:30 p.m. Sunday night, and most of the damage was done in about 20 minutes. Centennial High School in Utica became a Red Cross storm shelter for those affected in Beaver Crossing and the surrounding area. That night, Cordova also suffered much damage. There were eight confirmed tornados, with two of them rated EF3, covering a path of about 20 miles. (Both, courtesy of Kevin Fisher.)

Two

Bee

Bee was established with the coming of the railroad in 1887, with land purchased from Pioneer Townsite Co., a subsidiary of the Chicago Northwestern Railroad. The village was named Bee because of its location in B Township. Many of the first settlers were of Irish and English descent, but many moved on, and people of Bohemian lineage began to make Bee their home. In 1887, Michael Dunigan deeded a quarter of a section to J.F. Goehner, who platted Bee. The first buildings were erected in 1887. The rail line that created Bee was abandoned in 1962. John Herrold from Bee remembers the blizzard of 1888. Due to illness, he did not attend school on January 12, 1888, but his sister and neighbor did. At noon, a strong northwest wind began to blow, and soon, a full blizzard was upon them. "Our neighbor stopped by about 3:30, asking to hitch our team up to the sled to get the girls. Father said we would have to walk along the fence because the horses would not face the north wind. They found the girls along with the teacher and 18 students." (Courtesy of the Seward County Historical Society.)

Bee Township was, and is, mainly a farming area producing corn, milo, hay, and some wheat. Later, soybeans were added. A bank was started along with the new town but closed, as so many did in the 1930s. It did open later and continued until the early 1960s. The Downing family and some of the other families continued to farm on land obtained early in the 1860s. (Courtesy of the Seward County Historical Society.)

This brick building on Main Street was built when the Modern Woodmen lodge was put upstairs. This view is looking west and shows the elevators that replaced the train depot. The grain produced in the area is now trucked out. Many businesses lined the streets over the years, including a lumberyard, retail stores, a hotel, a creamery, and a bank. For safety reasons, the building was torn down in the 1990s. (Courtesy of the Seward County Historical Society.)

Lou & MaryAnn's Bar is open 365 days a year, from 8:00 in the morning until 10:00 at night. After Lou retired from the military, he wanted to provide a place for everyone to sit down and eat a good meal with family and friends. The Friday-night fish fry has become an institution, with people coming from near and far. The fish served on Friday nights is imported from Norway. The building on the far left was erected in 1888 on the north of Elm Street. It once housed a tavern and later became a grocery store. In 1934, Joseph Vampla purchased it as a general store, with lockers for meat added later. The building on the eastern edge is the tavern Lou and MaryAnn purchased in 1974 and started their bar and food establishment in. (Courtesy of Linda Jacox.)

The post office location once housed a butcher shop, and the concrete block extension was the Vondra Poultry and Egg Station. On this spot stood a wooden building that was the Ruzicka Butcher Shop, built by Ben Ruzicka in 1917. In 1922, a fire demolished all of the wooden buildings in that block. In 1918, all public places were closed because of the Spanish influenza. During the 1950s, a "Free Show" was held in the lot next door. (Courtesy of Sandy Roberts.)

In 1938, Vlad Sobotka designed and built the unique auditorium known as the States Ballroom. Much of the work was done by the WPA. The 12-sided poured concrete building features a 25-foot dome ceiling and a hard maple floor. It is listed in the National Register of Historic Places. The opening ceremony dance was held in 1941. Jimmy Marvin & his Streamlined Swing band played. The largest dance ever held in the ballroom was in 1942, the Sunday Fireman's Picnic. Nine hundred twenty-two adult tickets at 45¢ each and sixty-eight season tickets, along with fifty-two children's tickets, at 15¢ each, were sold. On Saturday nights, the ballroom hosted dances, wedding receptions, and much more, and still does to this day. To keep up with maintenance and repairs many fundraisers have been held, and it has become a well-loved place in Seward County. (Courtesy of the Seward County Historical Society.)

Pictured are Bee fire chief Fred Vondra (left) and Frank Tichy participating in a parade with a donkey and a goat. Tichy was known as the "Jackass Man" since he raised jackasses, as he referred to them. He was an annual participant in the Seward Fourth of July parade sponsored by Suhr and Imig Insurance. As they made their way down the street, the announcer would say, "And now, Frank Tichy and his ass!" Tichy also had a miniature animal zoo in Bee, with nearly 50 kinds of animals, and belonged to a national miniature animal association. (Courtesy of the Seward County Historical Society.)

Three

CORDOVA

With the coming of the Fremont, Elkhorn & Missouri Valley Railroad in 1887, a town was platted by the Pioneer Town Site Co. in the southwest corner of Seward County. Originally called Hunkins, the US Post Office declined that submittal, saying it was too similar to another town in Nebraska named Hoskins, so it was changed to Cordova. The community and surrounding area were primarily settled by immigrants from Denmark and Germany. At its peak in the 1900s, the population reached nearly 300. The Chicago & Northwestern Railroad took over the line, and a group known as the Great Plains Railway valiantly tried to save the track when it was severely damaged by floods, but it was closed in 1976. In the 1930s, Cordova had a consolidated rural school that included buses—the first in the county and maybe in the state. (Courtesy of the Seward County Historical Society.)

In 1902, a cistern was dug and a hand pump installed. The following year, a well was drilled as a town water supply for the fire department and municipal uses. Most homeowners had their own wells until a pressure system was installed in 1969. The windmill prompted Cordova's motto, "The Winds of the Past Fan the days of the Future." Everyone pitches in when maintenance is needed. (Courtesy of the Seward County Historical Society.)

Every community in Seward County celebrated the Fourth of July with gusto. Here is a photograph of patrons observing the Fourth at Max Schroeder's Saloon in Cordova. Schroeder bought the saloon in 1903. He remodeled, and his big sign could be seen from the railroad, welcoming thirsty passengers. He also had an icehouse behind the saloon that was always filled to the top in the winter. (Courtesy of the Seward County Historical Society.)

Early history records two newspapers, doctors and dentists, a cream station, a hotel, a bank, and shops. The opera house, built in 1888 along with the businesses on the south side of Main Street, burned to the ground in 1911. A brick building was soon erected and is still standing today. In 1923, several of the businesses on the north side of the square were destroyed and again rebuilt. Shown is the north side of Main Street in 1912. (Courtesy of the Seward County Historical Society.)

In 1907, the citizens of Cordova decided to build a jail. The jail never saw much use to confine criminals. In fact, in the 1920s and 1930s, hobos who came to the area on the trains were fed and confined for the night in the tiny jail. In the 1960s, it was purchased by Darrol and Carol Larsen, who preserved it for the community. (Courtesy of the Seward County Historical Society.)

Cordova was named after Cordova in Spain. Most of the streets are named after characters in Homer's *Iliad*. Socrates, originally Spur 76A, was later named after the ancient Greek scholar. The north/south streets are Agamemnon, Menelaus, Helen, Nestor, and Achilles, who were Spartans or Sparta allies during the Trojan War. The east/west streets are Aeneas, Priam, Andromache, Hector, and Paris, who were all Trojans. This was in 1887–1888, and along the streets, as early as 1908, the wood sidewalks were replaced with brick walks, and hitching posts were removed. In 1934, the newspaper reported, "A number of men went to Seward to see if they could not get the road opened up across the Blue River north of town." In 1940, a bridge was built. (Both, author.)

Cheesy Smith's Creamery and its employees are pictured here. After milking and separating the cream from the milk, people would take their cream and sell it to the creamery. Before the 1890s, Smith had two men working for him who would haul a cream separator to area farms, unload it, separate the farmer's cream, and then load it back up. Later, most farmers had their own separators. This and egg money is what people bought their groceries with. Icehouses were very important in this process; they supplied the ice to keep the cream from souring before it was either processed into butter or shipped to larger creameries. Notice the cream cans standing in the background. By this time, nearby Seward had a huge creamery that was buying cream from local producers, as they were processing hundreds of pounds a day. (Courtesy of Mike Bristol.)

"The Great Pigeon Race of Cordova" was started as part of the bicentennial celebration in 1976. Something was needed to make the celebration unique, and pigeon races seemed to qualify. That first year, the Lincoln Racing Pigeon Club brought over 200 pigeons to Cordova, and on Jerry Larsen's command, the children opened their cages and turned them loose. It is always the children who open the cages and release the pigeons. After circling Cordova a couple of times, off they went toward home. People from all over Nebraska bring their birds to participate. Now, a rib cook-off and car show have been added to the celebration. The *Pigeon Poop Sheet* is a newssheet produced for the community of Cordova providing the local scoop. The pigeon races are held annually on a Sunday in July. (Courtesy of the Seward County Historical Society.)

Four

GARLAND, GERMANTOWN, LEAHY, OAK GROVE, AND SUCCESS

A few settlers had made their way on foot out to the glacial hills of what is now known as Germantown in the early 1880s. They were drawn by the beautiful hills, oak grove, and an occasional spring of clear water. A railroad was making its way west out of Lincoln to Seward through the settlement, and Germantown was formed. (Courtesy of the Seward County Historical Society.)

After World War I and the conflict with Germany, the town was renamed Garland after Ray Garland, who lost his life during the war. (Courtesy of Lowell Krueger.)

Many Germans and Czechoslovakians settled in the area because the hills and trees reminded them of their homeland. However, the glacial rocks made farming difficult. Germantown was platted by Hilard Frazier and sprang up almost immediately. Soon, there were grocery stores, blacksmiths, retail stores, a pool hall, and a theater. Shown is the town hall, which was torn down in 1958. (Courtesy of Lowell Krueger.)

With the coming of the railroad, settlers were finally not dependent on wagons hauling materials out to the new settlement. The railroad hauled freight and passengers from the east through Germantown and on out to Seward. The hills were so lofty that the engineers on these trains had to ride the brakes all the way down into Seward so the passengers would not slide off the seats as they rounded the curves. (Courtesy of Sherry Sielhan.)

As the people settled in this part of Seward County, it was predominantly a dairy region. Out of a successful industry, the Germantown Creamery emerged. Business was so good that soon after incorporating in 1892, the owners purchased new equipment for the processing of butter and cheese. In 1918, a second company, the Germantown Condensed Milk Co., incorporated. The company bought and sold milk products, eggs, poultry, and canned farm products. This company was one of the most flourishing businesses in the county. Approximately 10,000 pounds of milk were brought in daily. A carload of condensed milk per week was shipped out. The operation was sold in 1935 to Beatrice Foods, which eventually closed the Garland plant. (Courtesy of Lowell Krueger.)

As early as 1920, the Folly Theatre was listed among existing businesses. It was a grand little theater with a stage on the west wall. The Depression probably brought the end of the movies. Olga Westerhoff recalled it being used as a community center. Then it was used for farm shows. It sat empty through the 1940s, then someone bought the old theater and an empty grain elevator to the south and converted it all into a feed mill. On the stage, a feed mixer with a mill grinder was set up, and in the basement under the stage, there was a big cement tank that was kept full of molasses. When the name of the town was changed to Garland, the depot's name was changed as well. (Both, courtesy of the Seward County Historical Society.)

The Bank of Germantown was established in 1904. The bank building was erected in 1917. The four pillars were brought into town by wagons with teams of horses. The bank closed in the 1930s during the Depression. Joe Pankoke bought the old bank in 1978 at auction. The building was listed in the National Register of Historic Places in 1987. Pankoke sold the bank to Bob Reichel of Culver City, California (named after Harry Culver of Milford, Nebraska). Upon Reichel's death, the bank was donated to the village of Garland. Since then, Bob Kirkland reports many people have donated time and money to the restoration of the building. It is now used for meetings. (Both, courtesy of Bob and Myrna Kirkland.)

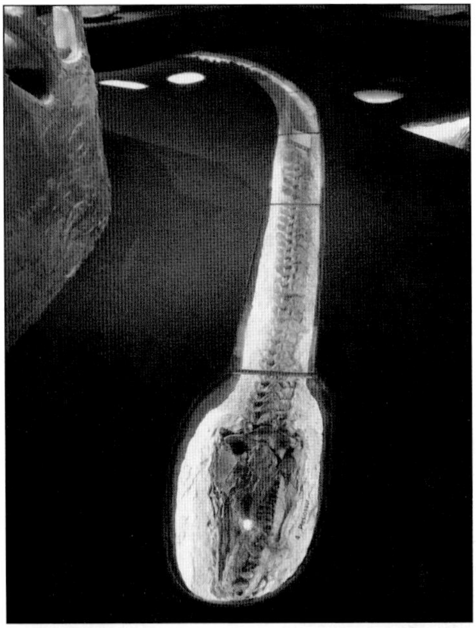

In 1955, parts of a fossil of a plesiosaur, including its gizzard stones, were found while working in the Greenhorn Lime Products quarry northeast of Garland. The fossil is now in the University Of Nebraska State Museum. Dr. C. Bertrand Schultz said it was known that they had lived here over 100 million years ago; however, one had never before been found. Greenhorn was started just a few years earlier by Carlyle Burdette Boyes. Bill Hartman worked with him and acquired the company in 1976. The limestone in Seward County is a part of the Greenhorn Ledge, which begins in Colorado and extends east to the Garland area. The use of lime on acid soils was widely practiced by Nebraska farmers. Bill Hartman ran this operation for many years and also has a dirt-moving business. (Left, courtesy of the University of Nebraska; below, courtesy of Bill Hartmann.)

A Pulitzer Prize winner and retired newspaper editor have lived on their acreage in "North Garland" since 1984. Ted Kooser won the 2000 Pulitzer Prize in poetry for his book *Delights and Shadows*. He served as the US poet laureate from 2004 to 2006, the first poet from the Midwest to be so honored. He is a presidential professor of poetry at the University of Nebraska–Lincoln and can be seen at times mowing grass on his orange tractor or painting a landscape in his corn crib–turned–art studio. Kooser is married to Kathleen Rutledge, editor of the *Lincoln Journal Star* from 2001 to 2007. She was the first woman to be named executive editor of a metro newspaper in the state. She worked for 30 years at the *Journal Star*, including 12 years as a statehouse reporter. (Both, courtesy of Ted and Kathleen Kooser.)

In the October 25, 1944, image at left, the Leahey elevator, which stood on the Burlington right of way just northeast of Seward, is being moved into Seward by the Engler Mill & Elevator Co. The Leahey elevator was a landmark in the community, where it stood for a half-century or more. It served exceptionally well in the days when grain was hauled to market by horse-drawn vehicles. The late Louis Meyer of Garland owned and operated it for many years before it was sold to Frank Engler of Seward. In William Smith's 1937 *History of Seward*, he states that Leahey had only an elevator and a mill that produced the Pride of Seward County flour. It was then moved into Seward. The stockyards at Leahey were dismantled two or three years ago. At one time, there was also a gas station there and the brick Leahey School. (Above, courtesy of Fran Lyons; left, courtesy of Marilyn Engler.)

The only remaining part of Oak Grove is the cemetery. It lies about two miles east of what might have been the community of Oak Grove. The community got its name from the oak groves in the area. According to W.W. Cox, the first settler was John Scott in 1864. Cox reports that in a year's time, it was a bustling settlement although never platted. The beautiful oak trees were cut down for log cabins, hauled to Lancaster to burn in the saltworks kilns, and used in building the state capitol. By 1867, according to historian Jane Graff, there was a judge—J.D. Maine—and G.B Hardenburg established a post office. Kirkham and Hughes had built a steam-powered sawmill. In 1875, Oak Grove was still on the map, but by 1908, it was gone. However, the nearby school retained the name. (Right, courtesy of the Seward County Historical Society; below, courtesy of Myrna Kirkland.)

Near the Seward/Butler County line are the reposted signs of a little country store community that was named Success. This little store flourished from the 1900s to about 1920, before automobiles and good roads diminished its need. It was also known for the Success Creamery. It had the appearance of a general store with a big plate-glass window, a high porch so that one could step off directly onto their wagon with cheese barrels, tobacco cutters, a coffee grinder, jars of penny candy, and more. At the "Leaving Success" sign is Don Suchy's place with an old-time "cave." Nearly everyone had one, and they were used to store produce and canned goods; they were also used as tornado shelters. Many a youngster can recall running to the cave along with their parents to seek shelter as a tornado spun nearby. (Both, author.)

Five

GOEHNER AND TAMORA

The Chicago & Northwestern Railroad wanted to expand its system from Fremont, Nebraska, where it was connected with the Union Pacific Railroad, to Superior, Nebraska, where it could connect with the Atchison, Topeka, & Santa Fe Railroad. A train route from Fremont to Superior happened to pass through Seward, already a town at that time. John F. Goehner, who lived in Seward, owned property southwest of Seward, which was located along the line from Fremont to Superior. Hence, the village of "Goehner" came into being. The road to establishing this community was not smooth, including a lawsuit. Goehner was platted and registered on September 26, 1887. Almost immediately, a number of businesses, churches, a school, and a growing population were thriving. (Courtesy of the Seward County Historical Society.)

The author is grateful to the University of Nebraska–Lincoln for this story about the first school near Goehner (although the university also states that the first actual school was a dugout built in 1871). A school, located a mile or so to the west, opened in 1873. When a town was built, the residents objected to their children having to walk out in the country to go to school, but attempts to have the building moved fell on deaf ears. One night, the schoolhouse was spirited into Goehner. No one seemed to know who hitched horses to it and dragged it down the road to a lot in town, but in the morning, it was there. In 1890, a two-story frame school was built. Later, a high school was built, with the first class graduating in 1923 and the last in 1945. (Courtesy of the Seward County Historical Society.)

This building housed the Seward Creamery at Goehner, as well as the hotel and the post office. The hotel was managed by Christian and Elizabeth Kennel, and the postmaster was Louis Wussler. Shown below with the postmaster's cart is Anna Marie Wussler Hansen. She was postmaster after her father died, from 1928 until 1954. Vic and Jodi Bartlett later bought the building, turning it into a restaurant known for its steaks and prime rib sandwiches. Vic was also the mayor of Goehner and was known for his enthusiastic job of emceeing the Goehner Melodrama. He and Jodi retired and sold the café. At one point, Biggerstaffs owned the restaurant where she developed and marketed a steak seasoning. In 2004, the business closed, and because of deterioration, the building was torn down. (Both, courtesy of the Seward County Historical Society.)

Albert Ebers first heard about the Grange as a student at the University of Nebraska in 1933 and that it was the best organization to protect farmers' interests. The Grange was organized in 1867 and was founded as an agricultural advocacy group. It was very active during the 1890s and was instrumental in the nomination of William Jennings Bryan for president. After graduating, Ebers returned and organized the Goehner Grange. In the 1930s, the drought and dustbowl era halted much activity, and it was not reorganized until 1940. Sears and Roebuck ran a national contest to see which Grange could come up with the best project to benefit its local community. Judges for the contest are shown below. Now 125 members strong, the Goehner Grange organized all of the area fire departments into the Seward County Rural Fire District. That year, it won seventh place nationally, and over the years won many top honors. Finally, it won first place, and was able to construct a new building with the winnings. (Left, courtesy of the Seward County Agricultural Society; below, courtesy of the Seward County Historical Society.)

After many years of hard work in the community of Goehner, the new building for the Grange was completed. It became the future home of the Goehner Melodrama, welcoming thousands of visitors to the community. Charter members of the Goehner Melodrama group included Roger Harpham, Caryl and Lloyd Schulz, Ralph Neilson, Pam and Cal Williams, and Sue Imig. This group produced their first melodrama in the year of Goehner's centennial, 1987. In the first year, six shows were given. Later, it rose to 22 performances a year, including pop and popcorn nights, Sunday dessert matinees, and prime rib dinner nights. The very first year, 3,577 people attended. Over $250,000 in student scholarships have been awarded over the years. Donations have been given to families in need, and many improvements on the Grange hall itself have been made. (Above, courtesy of the Seward County Historical Society; below, courtesy of Lorna Graff.)

Started in 1957, the Spaghetti Feed is always held the first Sunday in March and involves virtually the whole village. In 2019, the 62nd Goehner Fire Department Spaghetti Feed was held, with over 1,000 in attendance. The funds raised through this event are used to purchase fire department equipment, recertifications of first responders and emergency medical technicians, fire training sessions, and sponsoring summer ball teams. (Both, courtesy of Lorna Graff.)

Raised in Goehner, Julena Steinheider Duncombe attended Doane College with a major in mathematics and a minor in astronomy, and in 1945 began working at the US Naval Observatory. She worked as an observer and mathematician, analyzing observations of the sun, moon, planets, and stars. In 2016, the American Astronomical Society Solar Eclipse Task Force offered grants in Steinheider's name to promote careers in science to underrepresented groups. (Courtesy of Linda Jacox.)

The Chippewa Northwestern Railway is a 1:12 scale model train club that operates on second Sundays from June to October. Children and adults have a great experience riding the model train. A volunteer group operates and maintains the railway. The Chippewa Northwestern Railway was founded in 1975 by Jim Culver. The railroad operated at several different locations across southeastern Nebraska until finding a home in Goehner on the grounds of the Seward County Historical Museum in 1990. The railroad was built to provide hands-on experiences to those interested in the hobby of live steam railroading. It currently runs on over 1,800 feet of mainline track, in addition to numerous sidings. (Courtesy of the Seward County Historical Society.)

The Seward County Historical Society Museum was established in 1979 in Goehner. Doretta and Walter Goehner gave the land for the site as a memorial to their parents, J.F. and Dore Goehner. The village of Goehner was centrally located in Seward County and was deemed appropriate. The site is six and a half acres, and the campus includes the main building of artifacts with two more agriculture buildings, a 1915 schoolhouse, and a restored 1901 farmhouse. The museum operates with a board of directors and many volunteers. It hosts an annual car show and other events and is open on Sunday and Thursday afternoons. (Courtesy of the Seward County Historical Society.)

Tamora was established in 1876 and unincorporated in 1997. When the railroad extended its line from Seward to York in 1876, Tamora came into being. Legend has it that a name could not be decided upon, so they agreed to "talk about it tomorrow," which became "Ta'mora." The first post office was in Lafayette Weldon's dugout, but when moved, the name was established. Tamora had a grain elevator, a beautiful school, a bank, three churches, several factories, and more. (Courtesy of the Seward County Historical Society.)

John T. Pool was 13 years old when he, his mother, and his sister moved to Seward County in 1871. He filed a homestead claim two miles west and south of Tamora. He is credited with being Seward County's youngest and last homesteader. He married and lived in the place for 68 years. They had nine children, and all but one daughter moved away. After 100 years, not a trace of the farmstead is left. (Courtesy of Jane Graff.)

By 1882, three grain elevators had been built. In 1962, a modern elevator was built, followed by a feed-mill, replacing one that had burned. Out of this growth, the Blue Valley Coop, with 40 employees, developed and had more than 1,500 stockholders with assets of over $9 million. The grain elevators in Tamora were plagued with fires. In a tragic explosion, two Seward County men lost their lives in 1984. In 2019, there is still a strong grain elevator and coop business in Tamora. The wind turbine was installed in 2017 through a collaboration between the City of Seward and Bluestem Energy Solutions to aid in providing efficient electricity for Seward. (Above, courtesy of Caughlin Bohn; left, courtesy of Bluestem Energy Solutions.)

Six

Milford, Grover, Camden, Ruby, and West Mills

J.L. Davison first settled in nearby Camden, but while serving in the state legislature in 1864, he learned of a planned new road west. Davison relocated to the Milford crossing and started a road ranch and, soon, a mill. This new road ran right down the middle of the street as Milford grew. There was a constant stream of freight wagons and travelers coming up from Nebraska City to connect with the Oregon Trail. The second mill was built in 1883 after the first burned. In 1871, Seward was voted the county seat, and in 1872, Jacob Culver led a strong opposition to a proposed railroad through Milford, when it was then located in Seward. With these disappointments, along with a severe grasshopper plague in 1874, many early settlers sold to newly arriving Mennonite immigrants. In 1879, another rail line came in, with a station east across the river named Grover. (Courtesy of the Seward County Historical Society.)

Jacob Culver settled near Milford in 1869. He was postmaster and also partnered in a newspaper and the flour mill, then started bottling Shogo Lithia spring water from a spring near the Blue River in 1906. The water was sold nationwide and was popular in Nova Scotia and with the workers at the Panama Canal. "Shogo" came from a local Native American legend, and "Lithia" refers to lithium chloride. Two years later, Culver sold to Lincoln investors. As late as 1955, there was a listing in the Lincoln directory for Dr. Pepper Shogo Bottling Co. The old plant was torn down in 1921. (Courtesy of the Seward County Historical Society.)

Water from Lithia Springs near Milford was considered medicinal, and developers tried to market the area much like Saratoga Springs in New York. There was even a Milford Saratoga Hotel. In the 1880s, investors started building the Milford Health Spa and Sanitarium. Jacob Culver sold them 40 acres to build the five-story building, but it was not completed. Culver instead rented the complex to the state as a home for Civil War veterans. The state eventually purchased the building. (Courtesy of Ron Petsch.)

Stanley Matzke was born in 1898 in Seward County. He served in World War I and graduated from the University of Nebraska College of Law in 1924. He practiced law in Seward County until 1946. As a state senator, in 1941, he introduced a bill to establish the Nebraska Vocation-Technical School at Milford to be housed in the former soldiers and sailors home, which began operating that spring. In 1973, it became the Milford Campus of Southeast Community College. Today, there are nearly 300 graduates each year. (Courtesy of Ron Petsch.)

In the late 19th century, Frances Clark of Omaha began crusading to raise the age of consent from 10 or 12 and petitioned the Nebraska legislature to establish an "industrial home" for unwed mothers. The name was chosen because it was so socially taboo to be a young, unwed mother at the time. Jacob Culver took up the cause and convinced the City of Milford to donate 40 acres. In 1887, the legislature approved $15,000 to establish an institution for as many as 50 girls. The Nebraska Industrial Home operated east of Milford from 1889 until 1959. The children, when born, could be kept by the mother, adopted out, or sent to an orphanage. (Courtesy of the Seward County Historical Society.)

Riverside Park in Milford was utilized by many people from near and far. On the other side of the Blue River near Milford was the Easter Seal Camp, which was started nationally in 1919 to assist people with disabilities, especially children. The Milford camp was started in 1967. The Kiwanis operated it for a time, and then the Seward Woman's Club renovated the camp; it was widely used. However, a diesel train derailed near the site and fuel spilled, causing it to be deemed unsafe, and it was closed in the 1990s. (Courtesy of the Seward County Historical Society.)

Kenneth and Marie Dahle moved to Milford in 1947 and purchased the pottery factory, which grew into the national distribution of Klay Kraft Pottery items. He served in the US Navy before 1947, where he received a bachelor of science degree in mechanical engineering and was always inclined to develop and build things. In 1965, the Dahles relocated to Interstate 80, and Milton Erb took over the wholesale part of the concrete lawnware and some pottery ware. They delivered orders as far east as Galesburg, Illinois, west to North Platte, and South Dakota and Kansas. The business benefited from being on Highway 6, which had been paved several years earlier. Soon, things would again change when interstate highway system was formed. This new highway would be just three miles north of Milford. (Courtesy of the Seward County Historical Society.)

The interstate arrived in 1964, and the Dahles developed their new business with an "Old West" theme. They moved the Milford Pottery business into the old barn in 1966 and opened it to travelers. As they were putting the campground in, they built a huge Indian teepee around the restroom in 1967. The 32-room motel was completed and opened in 1969. The west-side service station was housed in a huge Conestoga wagon. The Dahles operated the business until 1997. (Courtesy of Dave Dahle.)

Everyone was excited when Charles Kuralt and his crew stopped in unexpectedly. Kuralt did a story about the pottery business on his radio program. The building was also featured in advertisements in *Time* and *Newsweek* magazines. During his spare time, Ken Dahle built two airplanes: the first from a kit and the second from his own design. Named the *Blue Sky*, it is now in the Seward County Historical Society Museum. (Courtesy of Dave Dahle.)

Don Strinz grew up on the family farm north of Milford. When he was 16, he spent a summer with his aunt and uncle in Canada and later published a book about this experience. It was the beginning of his love of the outdoors and the pioneer traditions. He and his wife, Donna, lived in Grand Island for nearly 20 years, where they joined the Nebraska Muzzle Loading Rifle Association. They then started making tipis and tents. They manufactured thousands of tipis (at one time over 700 per year) at the Milford location. Their tipis were part of the 1990 movie *Dances with Wolves* and the 2002 Olympics. With advancing technology, calls for tents and tipis dramatically dropped off. Don always had a word of advice: "Remember, Pointy Side Up!" (Courtesy of Donna Strinz.)

In 1862, the first bridge in the area was built by an overland freight company out of Nebraska City over the Blue River about five miles south of what is now Milford. A post office was established on the east bank of the river and named Camden. Stores and a hotel (which advertised as a resort) were built, and Thomas Graham started the first school in Seward County, with 27 students. At one time, Camden, Milford, and Seward all vied for the county seat, and all were even briefly considered for the state capital. Much drama ensued over choosing the county seat, with an arrest, an impeachment, and anger and resentment that carried over for the next 100 years. A short time after Camden was established, Davidson laid out a trail with a river crossing five miles north. The big Camden Mill was washed out in a flood in the 1880s, and businesses and residents slowly drifted away. By 1900, the post office was closed. (Courtesy of the Seward County Historical Society.)

Records show that around 1876, Grover was established in the area east of Milford. L.D. Chaddoch platted a town there in 1879 and offered to lay out 30 acres for town lots and give them free to anyone who would build a house. At first, the town was called East Milford and was built up after the new railroad came in 1879. The tracks did not cross the river yet, so all railroad business was done there. This little community applied for a post office in 1885, and it took care of the mail until 1905. The towns were connected by two bridges. Historian Eldon Hostetler reports that someone said one was for coming to Milford and the other was for going back. After 1886, the community wanted its own name, and asked for Grover. Initially, they had applied for Cleveland, but that had already been taken. Shortly, however, the railroad crossed the river into Milford, and business moved with the tracks. Grover declined. (Courtesy of the Seward County Historical Society.)

Samuel Long gave land for a village in 1883. The town was named after the depot agent's daughter Ruby. It was a stop on the railroad where local farmers could ship out their cream. A post office was established along with a general store. The Davis family shelled corn and took it to Seward to sell on the square for fuel. There was also a casket manufacturer in Ruby. The population peaked at about 75; however, by 1917, there were only 23 people in Ruby. (Daniel Morgen, the first settler in Seward County, staked a claim just north of Ruby along the river in 1858, but he was burned out and left.) By 1983, only the Ruby Coop and the town hall remained, with just two residents. However, there is a tradition carried on through 2019 of Dwaine Fosler riding his horse to Ruby every Election Day to cast his vote in the town hall. (Courtesy of the Seward County Historical Society.)

Though West Mills never became a village, it still established a school, had a sawmill, (adding a burr to grind grain), a post office, and the first baby born in Seward County. Also, Tommy West started a supply store in 1862, traveling the 82 miles once a month to Nebraska City for goods. These included powder, lead, percussion caps, barrels of whiskey, flour, bacon, tobacco, traps, and more. The Wests produced flour until 1910, but by 1930, hardly any traces of the mill were left. Tommy was remembered as kindhearted, and "the latch string of his cabin was always out," meaning that visitors were welcome. He and his boys were known to be proficient hunters, and he killed the last buffalo in Seward County. The West Mills community also had the dubious honor of a counterfeiter in the area. In 1879, Isaac Whitman was arrested for making silver half-dollars out of pewter and ground glass in a dugout factory near the mill. Pictured here are Alex and John West, nephews of Tommy West. (Courtesy of the Seward County Historical Society.)

Seven

Pleasant Dale

In 1864, the historic "Steam Wagon Road" ran through the valley of the present-day Pleasant Dale. The post office for Pleasant Dale was established in 1871 in a dugout on the side of Dunker Hill, and the Atchison & Nebraska Railroad was completed in 1879. By 1890, one hundred people lived in the town, with two general stores, an agricultural implement dealer, a grain market, and a saloon. In 1910, the railroad was relocated a half-mile south of town. According to W.W. Cox, in 1905, "In the beautiful little valley of Middle Creek in the southern part of the township stands the village that is so properly named—Pleasant Dale. The prairies were beautiful!" (Courtesy of Dale Nobbman.)

With an invalid wife and two small children, J.S. Dillenbeck left New York State and boarded an immigrant train to Lincoln, Nebraska. There, he fell in with a promoter and headed to Milford; the next year, he filed on one of the last homestead claims in Seward County, three miles east. As they were excavating for a bank-barn for the cattle, a new kind of earth was found, which attracted attention. After samples were sent to Denver, it was found to be gold and silver. In 1895, the rush was on. Of course, word had leaked out. Different ways of mining the precious metals were devised, but investors could not be found, and methods could not be agreed on, so the efforts were abandoned. (Both, courtesy of Dale Nobbman.)

By 1903, Pleasant Dale had an elevator, blacksmith, creamery, hardware store, barbershop, bank, and more. Several hotels were established. Plans for a local lumber yard were made in early 1890, and it was noted that 13 cars of lumber had arrived by rail, along with 13 cars of coal. In 1898, Ernest Uthe was reportedly putting in a new lumber yard. (Courtesy of Dale Nobbman.)

In 1915, Chris Uthe, his daughter Clara, and wife, Alvina, are shown with their vehicles. A few years before this picture was taken, merchandise would be delivered by dray wagons, the forerunner of semi-trucks. The dray wagon was a large, horse-drawn wagon used to haul merchandise from the depot south of Pleasant Dale into town. It was unloaded at the north end of Chris Uthe's building. (Courtesy of Dale Nobbman.)

Loretta Laymon came to Pleasant Dale from Indiana with her parents, who are buried in the Camden cemetery. Loretta married Joseph Laymon, and they had four children. Loretta's millinery business was based in her Pleasant Dale home, and she is pictured here with her daughter-in-law Mary. The millinery shop closed in 1922 when Loretta passed away. During the early days on the prairie, bonnets were made for protection from the relentless wind and hot sun. Often, material was at a premium and bonnets were made out of scraps. But still, people were mindful of proper headwear, and bonnets dominated women's fashion through the late 18th and 19th centuries. They were elaborately decorated with ribbons, lace, flowers, feathers, and trims. Eventually, hats and bonnets became so entrenched in women's fashion that it was deemed inappropriate for a woman to venture out in public without her hat and gloves. (Courtesy of Dale Nobbman.)

In October 1903, the Pleasant Dale bank safe was blown open with nitroglycerine, and $3,500 was stolen. Citizens were awakened by the blast, and action was taken. Shots were fired, but at the wrong buggy leaving town. With bullet holes in their buggy, the family was shaken but unharmed. The robbers got away. In June 1906, a jail was erected in Pleasant Dale, and a town marshal was put in place. Augustus Fougeron wore this badge for many years. The tiny jail was completed when its first occupant arrived—"A. Hobo," who was arrested for stealing rings and reselling them. In the 1920s, the jail was upset on Halloween by a group of trick-or-treaters, and in 1940, it was torn down. (Courtesy of Margie Fougeron.)

The Job and Elizabeth Reynolds family pioneered in southeastern Seward County; however, this picture shows that the telephone was a part of life early on. Pleasant Dale even has a mention of the telegraph as early as 1879. From 1910 to 1932, the telephone office was in the home of Cynthia Best in Pleasant Dale. She retired in 1932. It was reported by Lincoln Telephone & Telegraph that dial tones began to turn at Pleasant Dale on December 3, 1957, shortly after 10:00 a.m. In the early years, a telephone number was rung according to one's number; for instance, it could be three long rings and one short ring. These were run by "Central," the main switchboard in the telephone office, and each operator might have rung it just a bit differently. Party lines had as many as 7 to 10 parties on them, and only emergency calls were made at night. In 1977, Pleasant Dale was provided "one & four party" service, which meant customers could choose to have a private line or just four parties on their line. (Courtesy of Norma Whiteley.)

The Twin Lakes Wildlife Management Area near Pleasant Dale was proposed in 1963 by the Salt Valley Watershed Association, which was formed in 1952, and was completed in 1965. There was a very emotional hearing held at Pleasant Dale, as the construction of this dam would bury several family farms. The project was developed in 1972, with several homes being moved into Pleasant Dale. It was authorized for flood control on Salt Creek. (Courtesy of the Nebraska Game and Parks Commission.)

The Pleasant Dale prairies, from the very beginning, were appreciated and beloved. Lavender blooms in the spring and into midsummer, with butterfly milkweed and hundreds of other plants adding beauty. In the fall, the big bluestem and other grasses are colorful and tall. In 1981, a group concerned about preserving the prairie asked Gov. Charles Thone to sign a proclamation declaring October 18–25 Nebraska Prairie Appreciation Week. (Courtesy of the National Audobon Society.)

Eight

SEWARD

Robert Gale was the first homesteader in Seward County. He staked his claim in January 1863 (the seventh in Nebraska) and made his residence on the east edge of Seward in the spring of 1864. He was elected justice of the peace the following fall, and in 1865 was elected county surveyor until his death just a couple of years later. In 1865, Lewis Moffitt purchased land and built a two-room cabin for his family, which then served as a meeting place and lodging for newcomers. Lewis was also asked to be postmaster in 1867, and Seward was founded. (At this time, the county was called Greene, but it soon changed to Seward.) The town of Seward was surveyed and laid out by Thomas Graham in June 1868. The settlers in that first decade witnessed remarkable changes and growth. While some lived in dugouts, others built log cabins, and a few even had a frame house. (Courtesy of the Seward County Historical Society.)

Shown is the H.L. Boyes Mill, built after 1869. This would have been a bigger version than the first. The early sawmill was an asset to the community, and when they got the gristmill going again in 1869, it was important to be able to grind grain. Before this, people from Seward took their grain to the mill in Camden, as terms were not the best with Milford at the time. (Courtesy of the Seward County Historical Society.)

There were mills up and down the Blue River in Seward County. The beautiful Blue River was one of the assets that drew people to the area—it was clear and plentiful; however, it was difficult to keep the mills working because of floods and breakdowns. Into the 1930s, the dams played an important role, as they generated electricity for the area. Glen Clark, pictured here, was one of the caretakers of a mill along the river. (Courtesy of the Seward County Historical Society.)

Among the first settlers were W.W. Cox, Imlay, Clark, and Boyes, along with Roberts, who built the first frame building in 1868 and rented it to Beatty & Davis for a general store. There was soon a school, a mill, and a church. In 1870, O.T.B. Williams started a newspaper, a drugstore, and a blacksmith shop. Joel Tissue put up the first brick building. In 1869, there was a vote on the first rail bond, but it took until 1873 for the tracks to be laid. On the first passenger train came J.F. Goehner, who started the first of his stores. Claudius Jones started the first bank. John Zimmerer also relocated to Seward that year and started a hardware store. Kroeger's Shoe Store opened in the 1870s and continued in business until 2003. (Both, courtesy of the Seward County Historical Society.)

One of the real pests for people settling the prairie was the common house mouse, and during the 1870s, there were intense efforts to rid them. In 1866, when a vote was taken in Seward, there were only 14 cast; by the 1870s, there were a thousand inhabitants. Several members of the Morris family had moved here from Ohio; one of the brothers was an inventor, and had a patent on a better mousetrap. By 1876, the Morris brothers were producing nearly 40 mousetraps a day in Seward. Local banker Claudius Jones bought their patent and contracted with a Connecticut manufacturer to produce them. The first contract was for $2 million. (Courtesy of Jeanne Jones.)

According to O.T.B. Williams's "History of Seward," written in 1876, "The financial condition of the County was never more prosperous. Warrants on the general fund are nearly at par, the County being but little in debt. The poor farm is under good state of cultivation and the paupers well provided for." This photograph, taken in 2016, shows the 26-room frame building that was erected. A big barn that was still standing in 1936 burned down. It was estimated that the farm closed in 1940. Before then, there was no government assistance, so each county had a farm where those who needed to could work for food and shelter. Seward County's farm was right next to the Blue River and about a quarter mile south of a flour mill owned by the Heumann brothers from Seward. (Courtesy of the Seward County Historical Society.)

In the early days, the fairgrounds were south of Seward before moving over to the west of Seward. The Seward County Agricultural Society was organized in the summer of 1871 and was managed by Milton Langdon. The first county fair was in 1871. All of the buildings were destroyed in the tornado of 1913, but rebuilding started soon after. In 1915, William Jennings Bryan spoke at the fairgrounds. Thousands attended the barbecue. (Courtesy of the Seward County Historical Society.)

The fair has always been a showcase for the area's agricultural products, including livestock, poultry, and produce. While the decline of entries is linked with the decline in the number of farms, it is in no way indicative of a decline in importance. In the early days, horse racing was an important part of the entertainment. 4-H clubs are a huge part, and the entertainment includes carnivals, rodeos, the quilt guild show, exhibits, and entertainment. The wonderful Ag Pavilion was added in 1988, and the society has now added Harvest Hall. (Courtesy of the Seward County Agricultural Society.)

The brickyard that manufactured the bricks used to help build Seward was on South Columbia Avenue. It had a 150-foot smokestack (at the time, the tallest structure in the area). Thirty to forty people worked at the brickyard. Tragically, the worker shown here repairing the smokestack fell to his death a few minutes after this picture was taken. Some of the brick streets were laid as early as 1909. In 1909, the hitching posts were removed from downtown. The brickyard was closed in 1928. In 1998, new infrastructure was needed downtown, so a lot of the bricks were taken up, and a crew of volunteer residents helped clean them so they could be reused. (Courtesy of the Seward County Historical Society.)

Built in 1888 of brick manufactured in Seward, the Windsor Hotel was built for travelers. Among these were the traveling salesmen who came on the trains just a couple of blocks south and hired a dray wagon to haul their big trunks up the street to the hotel, where they showed their samples to area businessmen. According to Harold Davisson, the hotel had just one bathroom per floor and was known as a "bowl and pitcher hotel," meaning that there was a washbowl and a pitcher of water provided in each room. In 1958, the hotel was taken down. (Courtesy of the Seward County Historical Society.)

Fin de siècle is a French term meaning "end of century"; to describe something as a *fin de siècle* phenomenon invokes a sense of the old order ending and a new, radical departure. This was true at the turn of the 20th century, with new ideas challenging the Victorian ideals. The Fin de Siècle Club of Seward was organized in 1895. Founding members included Jessie Tishue-Langworthy and Winifred Cattle-Newton. (Courtesy of the Seward County Historical Society.)

The Fin de Siècle Club was very serious in its study and choice of programs in the early days. No refreshments were served, but the event of the year was the annual party, always held at the home of Jessie Tishue. This is a picture of the group celebrating its 50th anniversary in 1945. In October 1963, it was Seward's oldest club but was officially disbanded. (Courtesy of the Seward County Historical Society.)

John Frederick "J.F." Goehner traveled up the Missouri river to Seward in 1873. He established a dry goods store on the corner of Seventh and Seward Streets. J.F. and his friend John Zimmerer, who had a hardware store, planned a trip back to Germany, and J.F. asked his brother Peter to come and run this store. He did and stayed. Eventually, his son Ed took it over. The store was kept for nearly 100 years. J.F. started another store on Sixth and Seward, and later his son Fred started the store on Fifth and Seward. During his career in Seward, J.F. had a grain market, a farm, invested in land, helped form Protective Fire Insurance, represented the area in the state legislature, and worked to procure more railway lines to and through Seward with the town of Goehner being named after him. He and Peter contributed to the formation of Concordia University. (Courtesy of the Seward County Historical Society.)

Jane Graff related the history of telephones in the area. The Bell Company started an exchange in Seward in the 1880s, and in 1893, Billy Walker and his wife, Adeline, moved to Seward and took charge of the exchange. According to Adeline, they went to Seward in 1893 and had 26 telephones, of which only three were residential. There was one circuit of iron wire from Seward to Lincoln, and all calls to Omaha had to be repeated by a Lincoln operator. By 1905, they had about 800 phones. This was above Goehner hardware on the corner of Sixth and Seward Streets. An independent Seward Telephone Company was organized and was located above Jones National Bank and also operated exchanges in all the Seward County towns. They were fierce rivals, and many homes had two telephones in order to have complete service. Early operators were Fay Wood, Nellie Bye, and Jessie Landon. (Courtesy of Jay Cattle.)

August Heumann opened a tavern on the east side of the square in 1880. He came from Germany via Illinois. Heumann also had a farm and bought Coopers Mill and operated in until 1919. He also had an icehouse until 1922. His son Henry operated the tavern until 1956. Henry displayed many stuffed wildlife figures in the tavern, and families with children were welcome there. (Courtesy of Dan Blomenberg.)

H. Chapin and Dorothy Hand partnered in purchasing Ramsay Dairy with Max Anstine, developing Hand & Anstine Dairy. Dorothy at one time worked for Walter Gass, who manufactured and sold Linwood products by mail. In 1946, the Hands sold their share of the dairy and started Hand Grocery. In 1949, they began raising chinchillas, competing nationwide and selling them worldwide. The Hands won several championships, and their grandson Mark Miller has carried on the tradition, last winning in 2019. (Courtesy of Dan Blomenberg.)

In 1894, O.E. Bernbecker, H. Diers, J.F. Goehner, and Pete Goehner offered funding to win the placement of the proposed Evangelical Lutheran School Teachers Seminary in Seward, and what was to become Concordia University was established. Rev. George Weller, who was serving in Marysville (near Staplehurst), became the first director and continued until 1914. Concordia faculty defended the school's patriotism when its German ties were questioned during World War I, and students fought and served in both world wars. Growth ebbed and flowed as Concordia and Seward struggled through World War I, the Depression, and World War II. By the 1960s, the campus covered 100 acres and included 11 education buildings and 10 dorms. (Courtesy of Concordia University.)

In the 1970s, Concordia added liberal arts courses and majors, such as art, music, business, and computer science. Concordia is fully accredited and offers coeducational opportunities today to some 1,200 students on campus, more than 70 undergraduate programs, and 13 graduate programs. (Courtesy of Concordia University.)

After the first wood courthouse on Seventh Street burned down, the Seward County Courthouse was housed above one of the shops on north Seward Street, west of Sixth Street. The city's founder, Lewis Moffitt, had willed his 360 acres to the City of Seward upon his wife, Mary's, death. As they were deliberating plans for the courthouse, Mary gave the farm to the city to help move forward. The first county sheriff was elected in 1865, and the first murder was committed in 1876, followed by another in 1878. Building the new courthouse began in 1905. (Courtesy of the Seward County Historical Society.)

The courthouse lawn has been used for many things, including a market square with a gazebo for a band, a farmer's market, and Memorial Day and Fourth of July celebrations. When the Boy Scouts came home after a hike to Kansas, they camped on the square. The courthouse and downtown Seward are listed in the National Register of Historic Places. (Courtesy of Dan Blomenberg.)

The new Seward County Justice Center was built in 2016 at 261 South Eighth Street. It houses the county sheriff's office, along with the Seward County attorney's office, the district and county courts, and the public defender and probation offices, along with the county jail. The new building was needed for more space in the jail, more office space, and courtrooms. Security has been greatly enhanced, and new technology was implemented. The first county jail was near the old courthouse site between Sixth and Seventh Streets. The actual jail was just a tiny building next to it, described as a lockdown box, and it was moved in 1905 to the newly built quarters at Eighth and Main Streets. This facility served from 1908 through 1978 and was torn down in 1986. That whole block was included in the Moffitt estate. (Courtesy of Linda Jacox.)

Henry Campbell established Campbell's Seed House in 1913 and sold to his sons Walter and Charles in 1938. Jane Graff records it as being established in 1909 in a coal/ice house next door to the location shown here. Henry continued to build up the seed trade, and seed cleaning equipment was installed. After Walter and Charles bought the business, they added fertilizer and chemicals. They were the second in the state to sell anhydrous ammonia. In 1945, the brothers erected a new conditioning building of brick and installed a new mill capable of cleaning any kind of seed. After Walter and Charles retired, grandson Paul and great-grandson Mike continued the family business. The old wood-frame seed house was torn down, and in 2016, Bottle Rocket Brewing opened a craft-beer establishment in the old brick structure. (Courtesy of Duff Campbell.)

In 1913, a tornado struck Seward a little before 6:00 p.m., taking eight lives and injuring more than 30 people. It destroyed more than a third of the town. Many residences were destroyed, but it did not directly strike the business section of Seward. The deaths were commemorated by black crepe on many of the business doors. Newspapers reported that donations, assistance, and rebuilding started almost as soon as the tragedy struck. Someone had talked to a worker from a butcher shop, and he stated that as soon as he got home, he noticed a peculiar cloud; when he went to the back door, he saw bricks and debris flying through the air. He and his wife both grabbed a daughter and headed for the cellar. Not a minute after they got down, the tornado took their home. Several farms west of town had all of their buildings stripped, and all of the buildings were swept away on the fairgrounds. Eight doctors worked through the night, and the heavy rains made searching for survivors very difficult. (Both, courtesy of the Seward County Historical Society.)

In the late 1870s, J.C. Thomas and several of his sons formed their own band along with other community members. During the 1880s and 1890s, the band was quite popular, playing for presidential campaigns, weddings, and county fairs, and also performing outside the county. In the early 1900s, the Seward Musical Association was organized and became one of the leading bands in the state. It was later named the Seward Municipal Band. (Courtesy of the Seward Municipal Band.)

In 1934, the Seward Band played its first concert in the newly constructed Rosebowl. The land was given to the city by Mayor George Thomas, son of J.C. Thomas, and the old Wickersham livery stable, Fleesner Poultry, and Jake Imig's Bottling Works were taken down. The Bottling Works was then located in the next block over to the west. (Courtesy of Duff Campbell.)

Over 130 years later, the band is one of the last remaining and longest-running community bands in the state to hold weekly concerts. The women's band and men's band are pictured here in the late 19th century. Now the band is made up of a diverse group of individuals. Ages range from eighth grade to those who have played for 30 years or more. Often, musicians come from surrounding counties to play. Each year, they come together for 12 weeks in the summer to provide entertainment for the community. Each concert is well attended. (Both, courtesy of the Seward Municipal Band.)

Bill Dowding remembers swimming where Plum Creek joined the Blue River at the south end of Columbia Street. The creeks were clear and sandy-bottomed, and the clams were plentiful. During the 1890s and early 1900s, the boys kept to themselves, and sometimes, the girls would find another spot. The most daring of the boys would dive into the Blue River off the big bridge, but after three boys drowned one summer, a group formed to build a pool for all to use safely. (Both, courtesy of the Seward County Historical Society.)

The Seward Amusement Group formed, and a pool plus a dance hall was built. It opened on July 4, 1919. The lower level was the bathhouse, where people changed into their suits, or patrons could rent one for 15¢. The upper level was for dances. O.K. Jones was one of the leading bands to perform. The Seward Amusement Park building was torn down, and the new Dowding Municipal Pool opened on July 3, 2004. It was named for Bill Dowding, who was called "Public Servant Number One." (Courtesy of the Seward County Historical Society.)

The theater known as the Rivoli has operated continuously for 100 years. This old photograph shows the initials "HTH" on the building, which stands for Henry T. Hayes, who built the theater in 1919. Several people operated it before Chuck and Julie Wisehart took it over in the 1980s. The old marquee had to be removed when the street was widened. The smokestack in the rear of the building was for the heating plant for the courthouse. A tunnel ran underground with pipes carrying heat over to the courthouse. Sewardites have fond memories of movie money redeemable at local merchants. Edna Dierberger played piano for the silent moves, but the magnificent large organ that was in the pit was seldom used. The murals on the walls were made by an artist during the Depression. In recent years, the theater has added digital, 3-D, and another theater. (Courtesy of Julie Wisehart.)

The old Chautauqua Park in Seward is the location of the current Nebraska National Guard Museum. It hosted Red Path Chautauqua events from the turn of the 20th century until the late 1920s. Chautauqua was an adult education movement in the United States in the late 19th and early 20th centuries. Following World War II, the adjutant general, Guy Henninger, convinced Gov. Val Peterson to invest in an armory building. The federal government developed a nationwide armory building program in 1950. Nebraska added 17 armories from 1954 to 1956. The armory was dedicated in 1957, and the first unit to occupy it was Headquarters Company 2nd Battalion, 134th Infantry Regiment. The last unit left in 2014. The armory serves today as the Nebraska National Guard Museum, to tell the history and heritage of the Nebraska National Guard since its founding in 1854, honoring the service of Nebraska soldiers and airmen. (Above, courtesy of Jerry Meyer; below, courtesy of Ben Hughes.)

In 1896, a number of property owners formed an organization to provide fire insurance at a lower cost. At that time, many of the buildings were still made of wood frames, and fire was a constant threat. Among the founding members were John Zimmerer, J.F. Goehner, and Sam Oaks. George Merriam was secretary until he was murdered on the streets of Seward by his son in law. Merriam was replaced by Harry Graff. When Marcia Frevert moved to Seward in 1919, she was hired by the association. She remembers one story about a board member who had no patience with interfering auditors, so he took all the company's books and burned them. Protective Fire Insurance was in the YMCA building in the 1970s, and later relocated to Lincoln. Below, Protective Fire Insurance employees stand in front of the company's window. J.F. Goehner's daughter Doretta is second from right in the second row. She worked for the company for many years. (Both, courtesy of Marty Bender.)

In 1957, Protective Fire Insurance was completely restructured, and in 1972, Cletus Bender reported assets just under $5 million. Pictured here from left to right are (first row) Burdette Reling and Cletus Bender; (second row) Paul Colburn, unidentified, and Alvin Suhr. (Courtesy of Marty Bender.)

John M. Hughes moved to Seward in 1893. A builder by trade, he had come to work on a mansion for a banker, and at his death in 1918, had established a reputation of excellence that he passed on to his four sons, pictured here from left to right: John R., H. Burr, Ben H., and Ted R. In 1921, a severe ice storm downed many of the electrical lines in the area. Burdette Boyes, director of the Blue River Power Company, asked Hughes Brothers for assistance. They accepted the challenge of developing cross arms, and the company was founded. They started with wood and moved into steel in 1927. (Courtesy of Hughes Brothers Inc.)

By 1934, Hughes Brothers participated in the production of the first 115 KV transmission line across the eastern two-thirds of Nebraska. Hughes Brothers has over 290 dedicated employees working in a 500,000-square-foot facility and celebrates its 100th anniversary in 2021. (Courtesy of Hughes Brothers Inc.)

During World War II, Hughes Brothers produced 1,507,071 wooden ammunition crates for the 105mm howitzer, the 155mm howitzer, and 81mm mortar. The majority of these were shipped to the Cornhusker Ammunition Plant in Grand Island. Hughes Brothers also produced other specialized products, including ship davits, support structures for artillery camouflage netting, parts for anti-tank mines, and canisters for the 75mm projectiles used in the Sherman tank. The largest specialized products manufactured during wartime production were monstrous support trusses for the airbase in Lincoln, Nebraska, and Buckley Air Field in Aurora, Colorado. The trusses were commissioned by the US government for several hangars used to house B29 Superfortress bombers. Hughes Brothers employees took a can-do attitude on specialized projects during World War II. (Courtesy of Hughes Brothers Inc.)

In 1915, Fred Kolterman relocated from Blair and invested in what was known as "the Racket Store" on West Seward Street. "Grandpa" Kolterman would give customers a metal dishpan to put their purchases in, and there was always a lot of racket. Later, he acquired the butcher shop to the east and expanded the store. In 1937, it became a member of the Ben Franklin chain, and a new front was installed. Kolterman's son Don rejoined the business after World War II. Later, the *Seward County Independent* office (which had its entrance on Sixth Street) was acquired, and the L-shape addition was formed. Don and his wife, Betty Jean, continued with the store, and later, their son Clark continued the business. The Koltermans were very involved in their community, served at every opportunity, and helped enhance the Fourth of July celebrations. Clark's twin brother Mark served two terms in the state legislature. (Both, courtesy of Jean Kolterman.)

Harold "Budd" Davisson was an entrepreneur, visionary, hard worker, world traveler, real estate investor, and marketer extraordinaire. In the 1930s, he took a job at the Seward City Mills, cleaning out the mud at the dam, and stayed for several years to help develop and promote Buddy Boy pancake flour and more. He then started Harold Davisson's Farm Supply. He and Claire were secretly married, as she was a school teacher, and teachers were not allowed to marry. They started a hen house and poultry business on Hillcrest using lumber he and Erle Smiley had salvaged from the Beaver Crossing Mill. They sold eggs, cleaned chickens, and developed feed. They expanded, "Having Everything for the Farmer, But Rain." In 1953, Davisson developed one of the best promotions ever—taking a basketball team to Seward, Alaska, for a game—traveling by bus all the way on the Alcan Highway. (Courtesy of the Seward County Historical Society.)

There were always exciting promotions for what was now called House of Davisson. In 1954, when KAWL radio went on the air in York, Davisson was one of its first customers, broadcasting for over 25 years. The contests and promotions reached far beyond imagination and hosted many VIPs and local celebrities. In 1951, the Davissons had built a bowling alley. They sold it in 1966 and built the skating rink next door. This venture was very labor-intensive, so they rented the space out and later sold it. It was difficult to top this all off, but Harold Davisson did. He built the "World's Largest Time Capsule" and dedicated it on the Fourth of July 1975, "to preserve the present for the future generations." It grew to be a mass of concrete and steel, 20 by 10 by 6 feet. Inside, there is a new Chevy Vega, a motorcycle, and memorabilia from many individuals and groups. It is to be opened in 2025. (Courtesy of the Seward County Historical Society.)

Paul "Biz" Rolfsmeier ran a dairy east of Seward and also was a cattle buyer. Biz thought he would like to actually process some of his products himself, so in 1955, he started the Rolfsmeier Dairy Store in Seward. His milk truck also supplied products in the area. The children of that era have fond memories of the ice-cream store. The store burned down in 1969 and was not rebuilt. (Courtesy of Kathy Baumbach.)

During this time, Biz Rolfsmeier had come to know a buyer from Iran and learned the Shah of Iran wanted to expand dairy cattle there to ensure having dairy products. Arrangements were made. Each animal weighed over 1,000 pounds, so weight, fuel, and other necessities were calculated. Several trips were made in 1969 and over the next couple of years, each load carrying about 80 animals. (Courtesy of Kathy Baumbach.)

Hickmanville was a small community about three miles north of Seward where families by the name of Hickman had settled together. When Seward was making plans for its first Fourth of July celebration, a flag was needed. Martha Hickman went through her fabric scraps and created a flag. The number of stars at the time was questionable, as states were being added frequently, and news did not always travel very fast. Martha was an ancestor of beloved fabric shop owner Marian Ramsey Fosler. She had her shop in Seward in the 1980s and 1990s. In 1967, Seward's youth council offered to help reinvigorate the Fourth of July celebration. Gov. J. James Exon designated Seward Nebraska's Fourth of July city, and thousands have since made it a tradition to attend. Clark Kolterman, who was involved with the event from the beginning, has served for over 50 years. (Above, courtesy of the Seward County Historical Society; below, courtesy of Clark Kolterman.)

Nine

Staplehurst and Marysville

Staplehurst is the only town with this name in America. Ebenezar Jull, who homesteaded along Lincoln Creek in 1873, established a post office in 1876. Because of good water and good timber near the Lincoln Creek and Blue River, a small settlement called Lone Tree, consisting of a store and a few homes, was already established when the railroad was built in 1879. When the post office was moved to the new station, Jull's daughter renamed it Staplehurst after their home in England. Soon, the homes and businesses from Marysville also moved to "the new railroad town." Staplehurst thrived from about 1900 to 1925. A dam was built on the Blue River just east of town in 1908. The mill had a water-powered turbine that provided electricity to the community. (Courtesy of the Seward County Historical Society.)

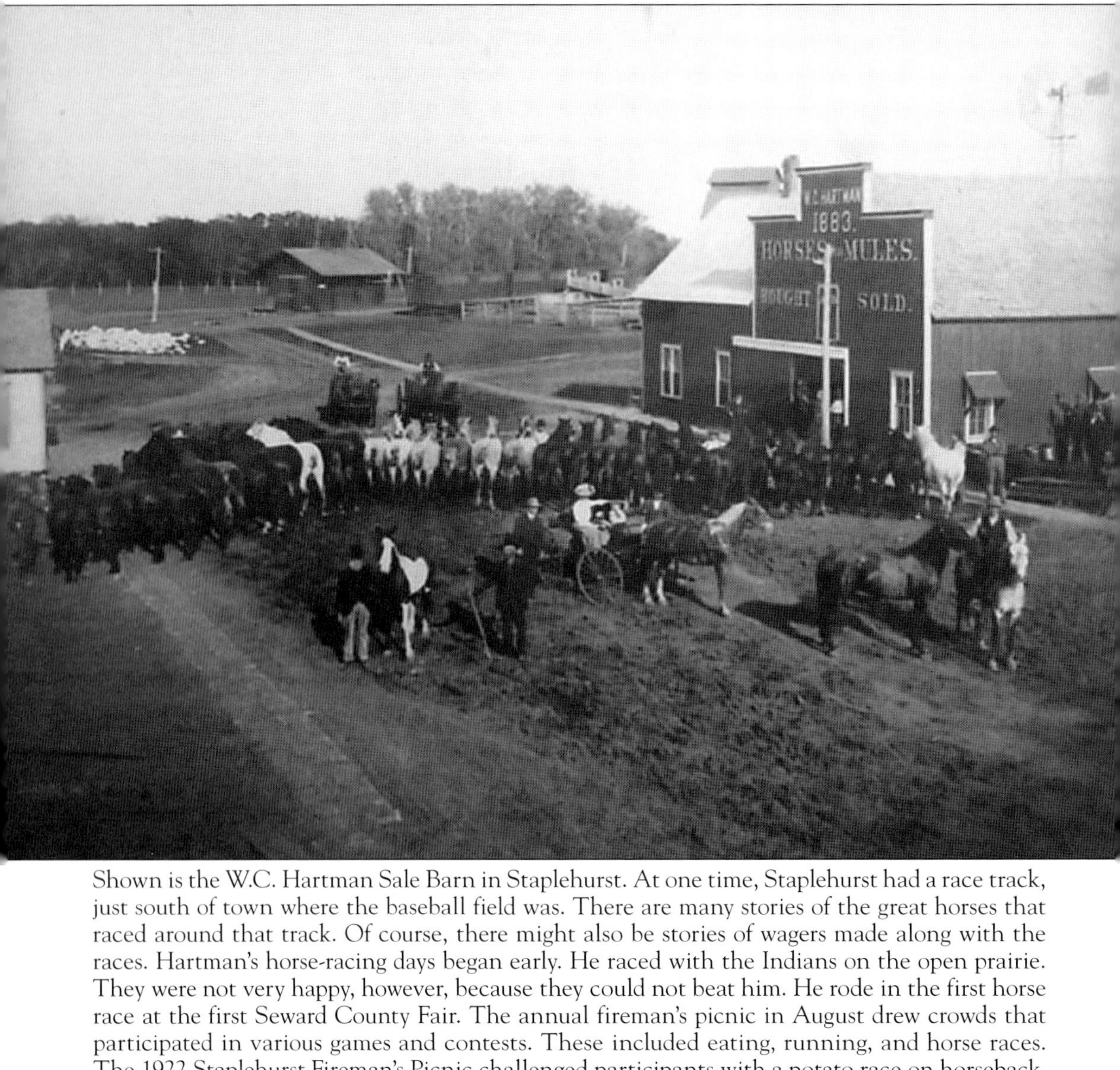

Shown is the W.C. Hartman Sale Barn in Staplehurst. At one time, Staplehurst had a race track, just south of town where the baseball field was. There are many stories of the great horses that raced around that track. Of course, there might also be stories of wagers made along with the races. Hartman's horse-racing days began early. He raced with the Indians on the open prairie. They were not very happy, however, because they could not beat him. He rode in the first horse race at the first Seward County Fair. The annual fireman's picnic in August drew crowds that participated in various games and contests. These included eating, running, and horse races. The 1922 Staplehurst Fireman's Picnic challenged participants with a potato race on horseback. (Courtesy of the Seward County Historical Society.)

The Henry H. Weller home in Staplehurst is seen here around 1903. From left to right are (first row) George, Fred, Edward, Ernest, and Louise; (second row) Lisette (Scheumann) Weller (wife of Henry), Clara, and Louise. After Henry married, he worked at odd jobs, including the general store that he eventually purchased for $700. (Courtesy of the Seward County Historical Society.)

Later, Henry H. Weller's son Henry J. joined him and bought his father out. Altogether, they operated this store for about 75 years. Henry H. Weller had come out to visit his brother George, who was pastor of the Lutheran church. Later, he and his parents relocated to Staplehurst. George later became the first director at Concordia College in Seward. (Courtesy of the Seward County Historical Society.)

Among the first things settlers on the prairie strove to do was start a school and a church. This was especially apparent in Staplehurst and Marysville. In the spring of 1871, the first church was built on Lincoln Creek near the Marysville Mill. This log church also served as the school. (Courtesy of the Seward County Historical Society.)

In 1878, a second church was built, and in 1888, a larger church was needed. The Evangelical Danish Lutheran Church was organized in 1877. The church pictured here was built in 1898. In 1964, the congregation voted to merge with a congregation from Pleasant Dale and formed the Faith Lutheran Church in Seward. After English settlers arrived, a Presbyterian church was organized in 1882. It officially closed in 1975. (Courtesy of Fran Lyons.)

Shown here is the interior of Meyer's General Store in Staplehurst. According to the 1976 "One Hundred Years History" booklet, some of the wives of old settlers like John Durland, John Varner, and Mose Mitchel used to smoke pipes along with the men. Sprague Wood loaded his family's organ into his wagon and took it to homes every Sunday for church service. At one time, there were nearly a dozen windmills in Staplehurst. (Courtesy of the Seward County Historical Society.)

In 1908, a dam was built half a mile east of town in order to provide electricity. In 1912, a celebration in honor of electricity for the town was held. This developed into an annual event. The first celebration was advertised by an auto caravan consisting of a brass band and 30 cars visiting every nearby town. It was huge, with a balloon ascension, merry-go-round, Ferris wheel, dances, and food. Staplehurst was blessed with a brass band and several musical groups. On January 1, 1926, from 8:30 p.m. to 10:30 p.m., Staplehurst put on a radio program broadcast by station KFAB. A chartered bus took the group to Lincoln. Messages in response to this performance were received from all over the United States. (Both, courtesy of the Seward County Historical Society.)

This is a 1913 photograph of Staplehurst boys at camp during World War I in El Paso, Texas. (Courtesy of the Seward County Historical Society.)

In 1890, the baseball diamond was east of town. Staplehurst has always been noted for good baseball, and several local players have moved up to the major leagues. In 1980, Staplehurst hosted the state semipro tournament, with 32 teams from around the state participating. In 1984, Staplehurst was awarded a trophy as an All-Nebraska Baseball Community. Shown is the baseball team of 1914. (Courtesy of the Seward County Historical Society.)

In 1870, Luke Agur built a water-powered mill on Lincoln Creek, and in a short time, a general store, a church, and a school were added. Before the rural mail routes were established, Marysville, a trading post three and a half miles west of present-day Staplehurst on Lincoln Creek, was a star route out of Staplehurst. Charles Bruce was the carrier and postmaster. Marysville was composed of Bruce's store and post office, the flour mill, and three homes. In 1890, Augur sold the mill to two Danes by the names of Rosenthal and Swanson, who ran it until 1897. When the railroad came through to the east, it was the beginning of the end. The mill burned in 1915 and was rebuilt in Staplehurst. The grinding stone from the mill has been preserved and is on display at the Seward County Fairgrounds. (Courtesy of Fran Lyons.)

A well-loved landmark still referred to as the "Marysville Church," Our Redeemer Lutheran Church is pictured here. The church and school include the horse barn behind the schoolhouse. Also included was the preacher's house, and in the back was the teacher's house. Many of the settlers came here in search of a place to worship as they chose. They started Zion Evangelical Lutheran Church in 1870. Reverend Gruber, who left Germany in 1839 because of religious intolerance, was called. He had also served at the Middle Creek Church near Oak Grove. The church and parsonage were built in 1874, with a new and larger church erected in 1879. The present church was built in 1917. (Courtesy of Fran Lyons.)

Ten
UTICA

Before the Village of Utica came to be, in 1877, one of the earliest settlers in the precinct was George Derby. He and his wife and family came from Iowa. George chose the east 80 acres; a daughter, Mert, the west 80 acres; and another daughter, Clare, took a timber claim one mile west. Mert and her father built a home together, but her part was on her claim. In her part of the house, she operated the first post office. They also had a sort of hotel with a little food and lodging, and the stop was referred to as Derbyville. The rails were completed in 1877. Standard and Jones erected the first building on the townsite and stocked it with merchandise. Then came a lumber yard, and soon, Fred "J.F." Goehner and a partner opened a second store and the rest followed. The precinct containing Utica was the last one settled in Seward County. (Courtesy of the Seward County Historical Society.)

Although settled several years after the first communities, Utica developed into a strong community and became the third largest in the county. By 1920, it had a population of nearly 1,000, and historian J.H. Waterman reported 34 businesses at this time. These included five general merchandise stores, such as the Kath & Harms store, shown here. (Courtesy of the Seward County Historical Society.)

In its early history, Main Street was advertised as "Utica's main street going north" and was originally called Wall Street. The photograph here looks from the north to the south (note the bandshell on the left). As of that time, there were two cream, flour, and feed stations; a dealer in poultry and eggs; two blacksmith shops; and four garages doing business. (Courtesy of the Seward County Historical Society.)

The village was incorporated in 1882. Its status as a typical rough frontier town may have been reflected in the village attorney's report in 1886, with fines collected for fighting, drunkenness, disturbing the peace, selling liquor to minors, prostitution, and carrying concealed weapons. In 1898, Carl Bereuter opened a blacksmith shop, which became a car dealership shortly after. His sons continued with the business and were active in the community. Rupert was chairman of the Community Improvement Association and worked with the group in consolidating the area schools, resulting in dedicating Centennial School in 1977. His son Douglas carried on the tradition of service by serving in the Nebraska legislature. He received his master's degree from Harvard in 1966 and served as an infantry and intelligence officer until 1965. He then served in the US House of Representatives from 1979 to 2004. (Both, courtesy of the Utica Historical Collection.)

Nearly all the Nebraska towns had a Home Guard, and they were subject to call if they were needed anywhere in the state. Utica had a well-trained group. The captain was at one time a captain at Wesleyan when it had military training. Utica had about 70 in its guard. During World War I, while the units of the National Guard and Army were gone, the Home Guard trained and remained at the ready for support of their community. (Courtesy of the Seward County Historical Society.)

In 1939, the *Utica Sun* newspaper reported that the First National Bank showed good assets, as attested by directors George Liggett, A.J. White, and Otto Thoene. George Liggett was president of the University of Nebraska Board of Regents in 1952 and died in 1964. The classic 1894 bank building with an opera house on the upper level survived the Depression and was robbed and badly damaged by a tornado in 1985; it was torn down. A modern facility was constructed. (Courtesy of the Seward County Historical Society.)

Utica is almost on the western border of Seward County and was created by the Burlington & Missouri Valley Railroad. Being that it was at the end of the line, it was named starting with "U," with Chief Utica of the Mohawks in mind. Utica was advertised as "the garden spot of the nation," with its level terrain and variety of crops. The building shown here was the oldest hotel in Utica. (Courtesy of the Utica Historical Collection.)

Shown is the horse-drawn water tank in 1898 in Utica. The following was written by Gene Czubowiz as a tribute to the 11 volunteer fire departments in Seward County: "Why do men like me volunteer? I guess it is because we feel that we are protecting our community, making it safer. It takes dedication and hard work to be a good fireman. If anyone thinks we're not scared, they're wrong. Anyone who isn't doesn't belong there." (Courtesy of the Utica Historical Collection.)

Fehlhafer's was started in 1957 as a Standard Oil service station and repair shop by Ewald Fehlhafer and the woman he calls his "best friend," his wife, Edith. The original business has grown into a major recycling operation handling automobiles, appliances, and any type of metal. (Courtesy of Ewald Fehlhafer.)

Fehlhafer's has become a major source for used auto parts, serving a wide customer base with its huge inventory. The company also has access to a nationwide parts locating service. Fehlhafer's is also known for recycling in Seward County; in 2019, they recycled approximately 1,202,520 aluminum beverage cans. Fehlhafer's Inc., along with Ewald's son Mike's business Breeza Industries, is very active and supportive in the community. (Courtesy of Ewald Fehlhafer.)

One of Kenneth "Kenny" Volzke's first enterprises was trapping skunks, keeping them in a pen in the farmyard until they had their thick winter coats, then drying the skins and selling them. The picture shows the pelts and the cooker where the tallow was cooked out so it could be used in oiling machinery. Kenny is on the left in this photograph from the 1950s. (Courtesy of Cheryl Volzke Richter.)

Kenny Volzke drills an irrigation well around 1955. The whole family—Kenny, Estella, Larry, Cheryl, Wayne, and even Toy the dog—drove to Enid, Oklahoma. It was sweltering hot. The drill rig was purchased, and Morris Perry, the first driller, came back to Nebraska with it. Because of the need for many irrigation wells, the crews often worked around the clock. Kenny founded the Volzke Corporation and was an entrepreneur and a legend in his creativity and problem-solving skills. (Courtesy of Cheryl Volzke Richter.)

Kenny Volzke (left) and Freddie Erks are pictured at the Sommer & Volzke Flying Service after hunting coyotes from the air. Coyotes were considered a nuisance to livestock, and a bounty was paid for them. (Courtesy of Cheryl Volzke Richter.)

The plane seen here flying upside down during an air show was flown by an aerobatic pilot. Loren "Mac" MacNeill was going to parachute from the plane. The announcer played up the drama, and when the dive out the door of the plane was made, the parachute did not open. Everyone was aghast. Without anyone knowing, Kenny Volzke had thrown out a dummy, and Mac was fine. People did not see the humor, and many left angry. Estella Volzke, Kenny's wife, never quite got over that incident, and that might have been the last air show on their private airstrip. (Courtesy of Cheryl Volzke Richter.)

Sylvia Virginia Zima Butzke has been the wife, sister in law, mother, and grandmother of Volzke Corporation employees, including Willie, Donnie, and Shawn Butzke. This fun picture was sent with a Christmas card showing her and her pet burro Murietta. (Courtesy of Cheryl Volzke Richter.)

The Flying V Ballroom in Utica was opened in 1971 by Kenny and Estella Volzke, and closed in 2004. Among the accommodations were a landing strip for light aircraft; a restaurant featuring Sunday fly-in buffet dinners; a party room for meetings, banquets and receptions; a public bar and lounge; and the ballroom, with a floating dance floor. Kenny Volzke was a trapper, inventor, farmer, pilot, and manufacturer. (Courtesy of the Seward County Historical Society.)

The Houchen family owned the pharmacy in Utica during the Depression. Ervin Houchen attended the University of Nebraska–Lincoln to train in pharmacy but decided not to pursue that career. Upon returning to Utica, he began working with the local book-repair person. Back then, towns often had a cobbler, blacksmith, auto and tire repair, and book-repair services. By the 1960s, the business had grown to a very respectable level. After retirement, Houchen sold the business in 1977 to H. Don and Connie Osborne of Omaha. Over the next 40 years, they grew Houchen Bindery into a nationwide resource. The following was included in an interview with Ervin Houchen's wife in 1989: "Ervin's aunt was a superintendent of schools and was interested in preserving books. This was before the Depression. So, we started with a glue pot and some scissors and paper cutters, and we'd go from town to town and hire kids to help repairing books." (Courtesy of Houchen Bindery.)